The Changing Role of
Rural Communities
in an Urbanizing World

Saskatchewan 1961-1990

The Changing Role of
Rural Communities
in an Urbanizing World

Saskatchewan 1961-1990

by

Jack C. Stabler
M.R. Olfert
Murray Fulton

Canadian Plains Research Center
University of Regina
1992

Canadian Plains Research Center
University of Regina
Regina, Saskatchewan S4S 0A2
Canada

∞

Printed on acid-free paper

Canadian Cataloguing in Publication Data

Main entry under title:

The Changing role of rural communities in an urbanizing world

(Canadian plains reports, ISSN 0384-8930 ; no. 8)
Includes bibliographical references.
ISBN 0-88977-069-7

1. Cities and towns – Saskatchewan. 2. Saskatchewan – Economic
conditions – 1945- .* 3. Rural development – Saskatchewan.
I. Stabler, J.C., 1935- II. Olfert, M.R. (Margaret Rose), 1950-
III. Fulton, Murray E. IV. University of Regina. Canadian Plains
Research Center. V. Series.

HN110.S25C42 1992   307.72'097124   C92-098018-X

74612

Cover Design: Brian Mlazgar, Agnes Bray
Printed and bound in Canada by Hignell Printing, Winnipeg, Manitoba

Contents

Figures   vi

Tables   vii

Summary   viii

Acknowledgements   x

1. The Setting   1

2. Central Place Theory   5

3. Data Sources and Methodology   9

    Data Sources   9

    Methodology   10

4. Previous Studies of Trade Centre Change in Saskatchewan   13

5. Trade Centre Evolution 1961-1990   17

    Introduction   17

    Overview of Changes in the Trade Centre System: 1961-1990   17

    Community Change and Agricultural Income   24

    Community Level Analysis   31

    Trade Centre Change and Access to Agricultural Inputs   38

6. Conclusions   43

    The Past   43

    The Future   44

Appendix   48

References   62

Figures

1. Community Shifts within Saskatchewan's Trade-Centre
   System, 1961-1990   19

2. Agricultural Economic Areas in Saskatchewan   27

3. Saskatchewan Trade Centres by Functional Hierarchy, 1961   40

4. Saskatchewan Trade Centres by Functional Hierarchy, 1981   41

5. Saskatchewan Trade Centres by Functional Hierarchy, 1990   42

Tables

1. n-Orders of Functions Provided by m-Levels of Centres   6

2. Changes in the Proportion of Trade Centres Among Classes,
   Saskatchewan, 1941-61   14

3. Changes in Number and Proportion of Trade Centres
   by Functional Class, Saskatchewan, 1941-61   15

4. Functional Classification – Saskatchewan Centres: 1961-1990   18

5. Summary Description of Saskatchewan Centres, 1961, 1981
   and 1990   20

6. Average Number of Businesses of Various Types in
   Saskatchewan Trade Centres – 1990   23

7. Saskatchewan Communities in Top Four Functional Categories   24

8. Number of Communities, by Functional Classification,
   in each Economic Area 1961, 1981, and 1990   26

9. Proportion of Communities Declining, Remaining Stable,
   or Growing by Period   28

10. Number and Percent of High Level Centres in Each Economic
    Area 1961, 1981, and 1990   30

11. Structural Characteristics of Communities that Remained
    in Cluster #4 in the 1981 to 1990 Period – 6 Communities   33

12. Structural Characteristics of Communities that Dropped
    from Cluster #4 to Cluster #3 in the 1981 to 1990 Period –
    16 Communities   34

13. Comparison of Communities that Retained Complete
    Shopping Centre Status Between 1981 and 1990 with
    Those that Declined to Partial Shopping Centre Status   36

Summary

Saskatchewan's communities continue to change in the functions they perform, the number of people and businesses they attract, and the way in which they relate to other centres within the province as well as those beyond provincial boundaries. At the time of settlement, spacing of communities was closely related to the grain distribution and transportation system. Changes in transportation as well as in production technology rendered the initial system of communities obsolete almost before it was fully in place. This report traces the evolution of the trade-centre system in Saskatchewan to the present and offers some explanation of the form the consolidation process has taken.

In the context of central place theory, 598 communities are grouped into six types of centres (in ascending order of sophistication in terms of the functions they perform) known as Minimum Convenience, Full Convenience, Partial Shopping, Complete Shopping, Secondary Wholesale-Retail, and Primary Wholesale-Retail centres. The resulting distribution of communities in 1990 is compared with the results of the same grouping procedure using 1961 and 1981 data.

Over the entire period the trend towards greater urbanization, with the largest centres gaining at the expense of the smaller places, is pervasive. In the earlier period, 1961 to 1981, this was primarily evident in the form of a large number of communities losing their Full Convenience status and some even their Partial Shopping centre status to become Minimum Convenience centres, the lowest level in the classification. The latter period, between 1981 and 1990, was distinguished from the former in that the erosion of trade-centre functions reached much higher up into the urban system with over two-thirds of the Complete Shopping centres slipping down to a lower level classification. A second notable difference was that the business functions of the large number of communities in the Minimum Convenience group (419) deteriorated to the point where there is no longer any single function whose presence can be counted on in these centres.

The ten largest centres are the main beneficiaries of population redistribution and growth. Even more dramatically, several high order business functions, specialized education, and specialized health care have become the near-exclusive preserve of the province's two major cities. Another fifty-two centres perform the role of regional shopping centres in their respective parts of the province and as such their viability is not seriously threatened. Below this, 117 communities are classified as Full Convenience centres and in this group there is perhaps some potential for viability.

The factors which determine that one community grows while others decline are many, complex, and often interrelated. Proximity to other centres, distance from provincial borders, strategic location on transportation routes, and other naturally occurring attributes all play a part in explaining any community's probability of success. In addition, however, the community's economic base, the impact of technological change, increases in incomes and changes in shopping preferences of the resident population are of major importance in determining the fortunes of Saskatchewan's communities. Communities in areas of the province where the economic base is relatively diversified have historically had a better chance of survival and growth than communities that serve primarily a grain economy. The presence of viable communities in turn contributes to the viability of the agricultural sector in the surrounding area by providing a source of off-farm employment income.

In this report we document changes in Saskatchewan's trade-centre system between 1961 and 1990. We also provide a general overview of some of the factors which have contributed to the observed changes.

Future research, based on the data collected for this study, will be devoted to an analysis at a finer level of detail of the specific factors that contribute to community viability. The results of this work will be published in a companion volume under the title *Restructuring Rural Saskatchewan: The Challenge of the 1990s.*

Acknowledgements

Funding for the research that made this report possible was provided by several agencies which we are pleased to acknowledge. In alphabetic order these agencies were:

Agriculture Canada: Policy Branch, Ottawa
Credit Union Central of Saskatchewan, Regina
Employment and Immigration Canada: Labour Market Services – Canadian Rural Transition, Ottawa

The authors would like to thank Agnes Bray and Brian Mlazgar of the Canadian Plains Research Center, University of Regina, for their work in preparing this book for publication. Capable research assistance was provided by Gillian Currie, Darren Filson, Michelle Stabler and Mitch Wensley.

1

The Setting

The small communities which dot the prairie landscape came into existence to serve the needs of the people who originally transformed these plains from grasslands into grain fields and cattle ranches. The spatial pattern of the trade-centre system that developed during the settlement era was influenced both by the early homestead acts, which fostered a dispersed pattern of individual farmsteads, and by the production, transportation and distribution technology of the early twentieth century.

Under the Dominion Lands Act of 1872 a settler could, for a fee of $10, file claim on 160 acres. Title was acquired by satisfying a three-year residency requirement. Although provision was made to purchase an additional quarter section adjacent to the homestead at a low price, even a half section proved to be a small unit on which to establish a viable operation in a semiarid region (Martin and Morton, 1938; Mackintosh, 1934).

The railroads that were built to carry the region's staple products to world markets provided lines within ten miles of virtually every farm. In Saskatchewan, when the system had reached its point of maximum expansion, the points to which farmers could deliver their grain were spaced at an average distance of only 7.4 miles. Other types of businesses to serve the farm trade were encouraged to locate at the grain stops. Through this process, the number of communities in Saskatchewan eventually reached 906. Clearly, most of these places were very small (Hodge, 1965).

Little did the settlers and developers realize that even as the settlement of the Prairies was nearing completion, technological advances were being made that would quickly render obsolete the system that they had built. Only the Depression of the 1930s and World War II postponed the inevitable secular adjustment that would have otherwise begun just as the settlement phase ended.

Adoption and implementation of new technologies accelerated

1

during the 1940s and have continued to the present with only occasional and temporary interruptions. The new technologies, which emphasized mechanization in place of previously more labour-intensive processes, dramatically affected the organization of activities conducted in rural settings and consequently, the communities that serve rural industries and consumers. Important in this respect were developments that facilitated the substitution of capital for labour in agriculture, and made it possible for fewer farmers to produce the same, or even a growing, volume of output (Britnell, 1939; Barger, 1942; Phillips, 1956; Fowke, 1957). Further contributing to the consolidation of agricultural holdings in the prairie region was the "quota system" under which the amount of grain that could be delivered for marketing was based on number of acres farmed rather than output per acre. Farmers were therefore encouraged both by technological progress and by marketing policies set by the Canadian Wheat Board to expand their land base (Furtan and Lee, 1977).

Transportation, communications and distribution activities were also affected by the development of new technologies. In the 1950s, for example, an ambitious program to update Saskatchewan's intercity road network was initiated. Paved intercity roads increased from 750 to 10,000 miles between 1951 and 1971. All-weather connecting gravel road mileage increased fourfold during the same interval (Saskatchewan Department of Highways records).

One of the first reorganizations to follow the improvement in access was that of the rural school system. Between 1951 and 1971, 2,750 schools in rural areas and small communities were closed (Saskatchewan Department of Education records). Grade school students were bussed into nearby communities while high school students travelled to regional high schools that were developed in larger, locally central communities.

Reorganization of the postal and rural telephone systems followed. Between the mid-1950s and 1980, 390 rural post offices were closed and 322 local telephone offices were converted from manual to dial exchanges (Canada Post and SaskTel personal communications). These reorganizations and consolidations eliminated many jobs in rural areas and small communities and transferred others to inter-mediate-size or large urban communities (Stabler, 1987).

The rural trade-centre system adapted to these changes. Smaller communities declined while the larger, centrally located, rural communities prospered from the consolidation process, at least initially, and expanded. Rural dwellers, both as consumers and producers, contributed to the pattern of concentration. As paved roads were extended into all regions of the province, shopping patterns shifted from the closest rural community to regional shopping centres where more stores, greater variety and sometimes better quality and lower prices were available. Bypassing of intermediate-size communities became common. Consequently, new commercial development increasingly occurred in the larger centres while it withered away in the small communities (Stabler and Williams, 1973).

The relative importance of specific influences affecting the structure of Saskatchewan's space-economy differed from one decade to the next, but for many years the sequence was complementary so that as the intensity of one influence diminished, another took its place. So it has gone for more than four decades.

For the most part, the adjustments of the 1950s, 1960s and 1970s were conducted within a generally prosperous environment. Prices received for Saskatchewan's basic commodities did fluctuate, of course, and in some years poor harvests coincided with low prices. But periods of prosperity followed. The 1980s have differed from previous decades in that world overproduction of small grains, coupled with the failure of GATT to restore order in international grain markets, has resulted in several successive years in which prices received were at or below the cost of production. Farm incomes have been supported by a succession of federal and federal-provincial relief and income support programs and an increasing number of farm families have taken off-farm jobs. Even with these additional measures, however, employment and income growth in Saskatchewan during the 1980s was less than half the rates observed during the two preceding decades. During the 1980s, decline, which was concentrated in small- and medium-sized communities in the 1960s and 1970s, reached much higher into the urban system. Only a very few large, diversified and centrally located communities escaped decline during the past decade.

The remainder of this study is devoted to an analysis of the evolution of Saskatchewan's urban hierarchy through the 1980s. In chapter two we discuss the conceptual framework, that of central place theory, within which the analysis is conducted. Chapter three identifies the data sources which describe the communities studied and summarizes the technique used to group communities into functional categories. Previous studies of Saskatchewan's urban hierarchy are summarized in chapter four. In chapter five we present our analysis of changes in the trade-centre system between 1961 and 1990. Our summary and conclusions form chapter six.

2

Central Place Theory

Central place theory is the theory most widely used to explain the number, size, and spacing of centres in a system of urban places. According to this theory, the role of the central place is to act as a service and distribution centre for its hinterland, providing its own, and the adjacent population, with goods and services. The reason why such functions are provided from central places is given by the concepts of the demand threshold and the range of the good. The threshold is defined in terms of the minimum level of population and income required to support a particular activity, while the range refers to the maximum area that the activity in question can serve from a particular place. The range is limited because transport costs raise the price of the item as distance from the central place increases. This is true regardless of whether the item is a good distributed from the centre or is one that customers have to travel to the centre to obtain.

Since the threshold and range will differ among various activities, a hierarchical spatial structure results in which the activity with the lowest threshold requirement is found in all central places. In today's context a gasoline service station would typify a service function with a low demand threshold. Only a small population is required to provide the level of demand necessary to support a gasoline station. Consequently, many exist and they are distributed widely — wherever a small concentration of population is found. Activities requiring a larger threshold, however, are found in fewer and larger places. Since the size of service areas vary directly with the size of centres, the complementary regions of small places are contained within those of larger places. Table 1 illustrates how n-orders of functions are provided by m-levels of centres.

The number of functions of each type required, and thus the number of centres of each size within the system, is largely a function of total population and income, while the spacing of centres is determined by population density and accessibility. Higher incomes and larger populations are associated with a greater number of functions.

The number of centres is directly related to population density but is inversely related to the quality of the region's transportation systems.

Table 1
n-Orders of Functions Provided by m-Levels of Centres

Order of Function	Level of Centre					
	Lowest	m-4	m-3	m-2	m-1	m
n						x
n-1					x	x
n-2				x	x	x
n-3			x	x	x	x
n-4		x	x	x	x	x
lowest	x	x	x	x	x	x

Referring to Table 1, it is apparent that the lowest level of centre would provide only the lowest order function. The next largest community, m-4, would also provide the lowest order function to its own and the immediately adjacent rural population. But the larger community also offers the next highest order function, n-4. These services are provided to its own residents plus the population contained within several adjacent centres of the lowest order and all of the rural population contained within this larger market area. Each successively higher order function, offered from increasingly higher level centres, is provided to all lower level centres and the rural populations within the ever larger market areas of the higher order functions. Often several functions will have approximately the same demand threshold and a similar range. Thus the number of functions of any given order will typically be greater than the single function implied in Table 1.

Distortions from the theoretical model occur in response to several common phenomena. Rugged topography or uneven resource distribution, for example, lead to uneven population distribution and to transport networks which provide better access to some areas than others. Further, the theory provides a better explanation of the functioning of centres in agricultural than in highly industrialized regions. The service centre role is more clearly apparent when there are few places of large size in a region. When there are several large centres of similar size there is a greater possibility of specialization by function, such as manufacturing or government for example, which may lead to a distortion of the urban size hierarchy.

In spite of these qualifications, the theory is the most useful one available for the analysis of trade-centre systems. No other theory stresses so much the fundamental interdependence between the community and the region within which it is located. Further, at the operational level, the theoretical relationships specified are capable of empirical verification.

Central place theory is well suited for the topic at hand. Saskatchewan's economy was initially based on agriculture and this sector still provides the basis for much of the employment and income generated within the province. The majority of Saskatchewan's communities came into existence to serve the needs of the agricultural economy. Indeed, their locations were determined primarily by the transportation requirements of the grain industry. Most Saskatchewan communities still perform an agricultural trade-centre function. In addition, there are no really large cities in the province. The largest, Saskatoon and Regina, have specialized to a limited extent but both still are dominant communities in the province's trade-centre system.

Central place theory describes a system in equilibrium; that is, one in which population size and distribution, income and technology are unchanging. Because of this property it is referred to as a static equilibrium theory. This might at first appear as a drawback because we know that technology, income and consequently the province's total population and its distribution have changed significantly over the past several decades. The apparent limitations of a static theory are circumvented to a degree by performing what is referred to as comparative static analysis. In this form of analysis the characteristics of the system are completely identified at two points in time. In a dynamic economy the system would be expected to differ at dates separated by several years. These differences then become the focus of attention and an effort is made to interpret and explain the changes noted by reference to evolving technologies, improvements in transportation, rising incomes, behaviour of people as both consumers and producers, as well as other influences which may become apparent in the conduct of the analysis. (A thorough discussion of central place theory is available in Berry et al., 1988.)

The study of Saskatchewan's trade-centre system in the following chapters is conducted using central place theory and a comparative static approach.

3

Data Sources and Methodology

Data Sources

Communities included in this analysis were those 598 incorporated and unincorporated places which, in 1961, had fifty or more inhabitants. For this group of communities data were initially collected, and the analysis performed, for 1961 to 1981 in a study completed in the mid-1980s (Stabler, 1987). The same communities were subsequently included in a study of the 1981-90 period which forms the basis of this report.

Data describing each community were collected from a variety of sources. Information on the number of business outlets in the communities were obtained primarily from the Dun and Bradstreet *Reference Book*. The businesses are listed according to individual Standard Industrial Classification (SIC) codes. These SIC codes were grouped into thirty-six categories representing groups of businesses commonly found in prairie centres. The number of businesses in each group were then tabulated for each of the 598 communities for 1961, 1981 and 1990.

Several business functions were not adequately represented in Dun and Bradstreet. Further, data for infrastructure and some professional services are not available from this source. Information on the number of grain elevators, banks, credit unions, other financial institutions, dentists, lawyers, doctors, hospital beds, special care beds, elementary and high school enrolments, postsecondary educational institutions, and real estate offices were obtained from other sources. Professional associations provided data on the location of their members. Banks and the Saskatchewan Credit Union Central contributed a list of the number of their outlets in each community. Education and health care data originated with provincial government departments. The number of elevators and elevator capacity is described in publications from the Canadian Grain Commission. Community profiles, prepared by the provincial Department of Rural Development, provided supplementary information for some of the communities.

Population data and age distributions of the populations were obtained primarily from Saskatchewan Health's *Covered Population* statistics and were in some cases augmented with, or crosschecked against, census records.

Information regarding commuting distances of persons working in, but not residents of, Saskatchewan's largest thirty-one centres was obtained from special tabulations of the 1981 census. Commuting distances were calculated as weighted averages for people working in these thirty-one communities but living outside the centre of their employment.

In addition to the statistical data, interviews were conducted in some three dozen rural communities over an eight-month period. Groups ranging in size from four to fourteen people were assembled with the help of extension agrologists employed by the Department of Rural Development, to represent community leaders, town administrators, economic development officers, rural municipality administrators, and the business community. Preliminary results of the statistical analyses were presented to these groups to obtain their input and impressions of the accuracy and validity of the data describing their community, as well as to provide insights into the interpretation of the data. Several dozen additional communities were visited, without interviews, both as a crosscheck on the statistical profiles and to provide additional, more subjective interpretation.

All of the tables and figures in this report were derived from these data bases unless otherwise indicated. Sources are not identified on each individual presentation, however, because they are typically too numerous.

Methodology

In order to group the communities in the study into functional categories a cluster analysis program was utilized. Cluster analysis is a classificatory technique designed to select subsets of mutually similar objects from the set of all such objects. In this case the task is to select subsets of functionally similar communities from the entire set of 598 communities. Each community is described by a comprehensive set of attributes, all of which are considered simultaneously in the classification scheme. The relevant quantifiable characteristics of a community include population size (and age distribution), the entire array of business functions, and the additional infrastructure as described under data sources in the preceding section. Through a complex computer algorithm, the program is able to evaluate, compare and ultimately group centres on the basis of their similarities in terms of the dimensions in which they are described.

For the cluster analysis, the raw data were standardized prior to clustering in order to facilitate comparison of such disparate variables as population size and number of grocery stores. A similarity matrix was subsequently computed where the coefficients represent the distance between communities. Clusters were formed using Ward's (or Orloci's) method which minimizes the distance between the subject and its group centroid as fusion proceeds. (A technical description of this procedure is found in Wishart, 1987.) Other methods of clustering were also evaluated.

After the initial formation of clusters, the compactness and distinctness of the clusters were tested. An iterative relocation option was utilized to find local optima and a test of whether these local optima represented global efficiency was performed by reinitiating the iterative relocation procedure from several radically different starting classifications. The local optima were found to be very robust. The validity of the groupings was further tested using a t-test for the significance of the differences in the means of the population size and the number of business outlets of adjacent clusters. Finally, the classifications were evaluated using multiple discriminant analysis. In all cases the groups were found to be statistically valid.

This technique resulted in the formation of six distinct clusters for the 1990 data as well as for the two preceding time periods. Given the theoretical context for the analysis, these six clusters are taken to represent the functional categories in a trade-centre hierarchy as described in chapter two. These categories are commonly described as Minimum Convenience, Full Convenience, Partial Shopping, Complete Shopping, Secondary Wholesale-Retail, and Primary Wholesale-Retail centres.

Minimum convenience centres are conventionally considered to be the smallest, and functionally simplest, trade centres offering a small core of basics such as gasoline and groceries, that require a relatively small-size market area. In addition, a limited number of less frequently used goods and services may be available. Full Convenience centres are those in the next tier and they would perform all the functions of a Minimum Convenience centre and in addition also typically offer a set of goods and services, such as general merchandise and implement dealer outlets, requiring a larger size market area. Each subsequent tier in the hierarchy (Partial Shopping, Complete Shopping, Secondary Wholesale-Retail, and Primary Wholesale-Retail) performs all of the functions of the centres in the previous tiers and, in addition, offers more sophisticated goods and services that require larger market areas. The particular functions performed at each tier will vary somewhat over time and from one geographic area to the next, but the hierarchical structure of trade centres will persist because of the differential market areas required for different goods and services.

In the following chapters we use the data and computer programs just described to identify the way in which the structure of the trade centre system has changed through time. We also discuss the experience of groups of communities in terms of the importance of size, location, and functional characteristics.

4

Previous Studies of Trade Centre Change in Saskatchewan

$\mathbf{F}$arm consolidation, rural to urban migration, and the decline of small communities had become a common experience elsewhere in North America while Saskatchewan was still expanding. Several earlier studies refer to these events (Lively, 1932; Brunner, 1936; Anderson, 1950 and 1953). Much of this early research was in rural sociology and consisted primarily either of case studies or generalizations based on overviews of population or other census data.

The first in-depth study of rural communities in Saskatchewan and the relationship between their vitality and the activities conducted in their hinterland, was undertaken by a provincial royal commission in the 1950s (Saskatchewan, 1957). Based on case studies in southwestern Saskatchewan, hierarchical relationships between communities of different size were identified and the differential impact on communities of economic changes in their hinterlands were discussed. Although this was an impressive pioneering effort, it was conducted before computers became a standard tool in social science research. Consequently it did not use the massive data bases that have since become available and it failed to identify the systematic relationships between structure, function and location these data are capable of revealing.

The first really comprehensive analysis of Saskatchewan's trade-centre system was conducted by Gerald Hodge (1965, 1968). In his study, he attempted to quantitatively establish the extent to which change had occurred in the system between 1941 and 1961 and to identify the influences responsible for these changes.

Hodge's analysis included all incorporated and unincorporated communities in the province. He was able to identify 906 places in 1941, a number which had declined to 779 by 1961.

A full range of economic, demographic and infrastructure variables were used to describe the centres studied. Hodge used factor analysis to group communities into functional categories. Regression analysis was subsequently used to determine to what extent community differences, as indicated by the factor analysis, were related to trade-centre change. Although the particular approach used did not adequately identify causes of trade-centre decline, Hodge did observe a process of change that has in broad outline characterized the evolution of the trade-centre system during the following three decades. Three observations were of particular interest:

1. Trade centres ranking low in the retail service hierarchy at the beginning of the period lost rank more rapidly than higher ranking centres from 1941-61.

2. Between 1941 and 1961, the number of centres at both extremes of the retail service hierarchy increased relative to centres in the middle range of the hierarchy.

3. Where trade centres at the same class situated adjacent to one another were separated by less than the average spacing for the class in 1941, one or more of the centres experienced either relative or absolute decline by 1961.

A table from Hodge's 1965 article is reproduced here as Table 2. It identifies changes in the status of trade centres during the twenty years covered by his analysis.

Table 2
Changes in the Proportion of Trade Centres among Classes, Saskatchewan, 1941-61

Class of Centre 1941	Expired by 1961	Hamlet	Min. Conv.	Full Conv.	Part. Shop.	Comp. Shop.	Sec. W-R	Prim. W-R
				(percentages)				
New Centre (1942-51)	*48*	52						
Hamlet	46	*52*	02					
Min. Conv.	02	63	*27*	07	01			
Full Conv.		06	28	*39*	26	01		
Part. Shop.			02	19	*63*	16		
Compl. Shop.					12	*73*	15	
Secondary W-R							*100*	
Primary W-R								*100*

Source: Hodge, 1965: 96.

Referring to the table, if each centre existing in 1941 had retained its status during the following twenty years, all entries would appear as 100 on the principal diagonal running from the upper left corner to the bottom right corner. Since they did not, the reclassifications for 1961 are read along each row. For example, 39 percent of the communities classified as Full Convenience centres in 1941 retained that status in 1961. Twenty-six percent rose to Partial Shopping and one percent to Complete Shopping centre status. A slightly larger percentage declined, 28 to Minimum Convenience and 6 percent to Hamlet status.

The 1941-51 decade was the first time Saskatchewan experienced a net loss of trade centres. Between 1941 and 1951, sixty-nine new communities were founded but eighty-three expired. Between 1951 and 1961, the loss was greater — sixteen new centres were created, while 129 disappeared. Decline in trade-centre status was common as well. Between 1941 and 1951, 142 communities moved downward. In the following decade, 148 more declined.

Table 3
Changes in Number and Proportion of Trade Centres
by Functional Class, Saskatchewan, 1941-61

Type of Centre	1941		1951		1961		% Change 1941-61
	No.	%	No.	%	No.	%	
Primary Wholesale-Retail	2	0.2	2	0.2	2	0.3	0.0
Secondary Wholesale-Retail	5	0.6	8	0.9	9	1.2	80.0
Compl. Shopping	26	2.9	23	2.6	29	3.7	11.6
Partial Shopping	57	6.3	66	7.4	85	10.9	49.2
Full Convenience	171	18.9	169	18.9	100	12.7	-41.5
Min. Convenience	287	31.8	191	21.4	150	19.4	-47.8
Hamlet	358	39.3	433	48.6	404	51.8	12.8
All Trade Centres	906	100.0	892	100.0	779	100.0	-14.0

Source: Hodge, 1965: 95.

During the two decades covered in Hodge's study, there was some growth in the number of communities at the upper levels in the hierarchy. Secondary Wholesale-Retail centres increased from five to nine; Complete Shopping centres from twenty-six to twenty-nine and Partial Shopping centres from fifty-seven to eighty-five. Below the

Partial Shopping category, decline was common. Table 3, also from Hodge's 1965 article, identifies these changes.

As a generalization, growth in number, size and functional complexity was the more common experience for the Partial Shopping and higher level classifications, while decline in numbers and functional complexity was common below that.

Thus, as Hodge clearly demonstrated, consolidation of the trade-centre system began almost immediately after completion of the settlement era and gained momentum during the 1950s. The next chapter focusses on the experience between 1961 and 1990.

5

Trade Centre Evolution 1961-1990

Introduction

The data base and the methodology used for the study of trade centre change since 1961 differ somewhat from those used by Hodge.

To begin with, a smaller number of centres were chosen for this study. Our set of communities consist of those 598 incorporated and unincorporated places, which in 1961, had populations of fifty or more and which were also listed in the 1981 census. We observed, but excluded, forty unincorporated places which had populations in excess of fifty in 1961 but which were not listed in the 1981 census. Presumably, they had expired. The few communities that amalgamated during this period were treated as if they had been a single centre throughout.

Approximately 135 very small communities identified by Hodge in 1961 were excluded from our study because they had populations of fewer than fifty people and, after 1961, data were not systematically available for these places.

The method used for grouping the communities for 1961, 1981 and 1990 was cluster analysis as explained in chapter three.

One of the consequences of excluding the smallest communities and using a different methodology for grouping was the identification of six functional classifications whereas Hodge had identified a seventh, that of Hamlet.

Overview of Changes in the Trade-Centre System: 1961-1990

We begin by comparing the number of communities in each functional classification for 1961, 1981 and 1990. These comparisons are provided in Table 4. Between 1961 and 1981, a very substantial downward movement of communities in the middle categories occurred. In 1961, for example, there were 317 communities situated in the three clusters between the Secondary Wholesale-Retail level and the lowest functional classification, the Minimum Convenience centre. By 1981, the number occupying this interval had decreased to 188. During this time period, the number of communities in the top three categories was relatively stable.

Table 4
Functional Classification – Saskatchewan Centres: 1961-1990

Functional Classification	1961	1981	1990
Primary Wholesale-Retail	2	2	2
Secondary Wholesale-Retail	8	8	8
Complete Shopping centre	29	22	6
Partial Shopping centre	99	30	46
Full Convenience centre	189	136	117
Minimum Convenience centre	271	400	419

Between 1981 and 1990 there was some further downward movement of centres in the middle categories, but at a much slower rate. The number of communities in the three clusters between the Secondary Wholesale-Retail and the Minimum Convenience levels declined from 188 in 1981 to 169 in 1990. What is most striking about the latter period is the pronounced decline of communities which had Complete Shopping centre status in 1981 — only six of twenty-two centres (27 percent) remained in this category in 1990.

An additional consideration distinguishes both the 1961-81 and the 1981-90 periods from the twenty years studied by Hodge. That is, there were many fewer centres that rose in classification during the past three decades than between 1941 and 1961. Nearly all changes since 1961 have been downward. Explicit movements between groups are shown in Figure 1. In this figure, solid lines identify the number of communities remaining in the same classification between two dates (such as the twenty-one connecting the CSC blocks between 1961 and 1981) or declining (such as the eight connecting the CSC block in 1961 with the PSC block in 1981). Dashed lines show upward movement.

In Table 5 summary descriptions of the functional classifications for each of the dates utilized are provided. In this table, three figures appear under both the population and business outlets columns opposite each functional classification for each year. The middle number in each set is the mean value while the ones above and below

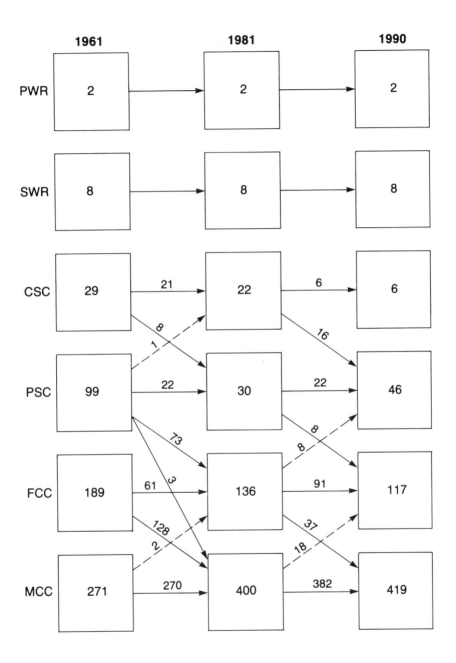

Figure 1. Community Shifts Within Saskatchewan's Trade-Centre System, 1961-1990.

identify the mean plus-and-minus one standard deviation respectively. For example, for Minimum Convenience centres, the average population size in 1961 was 121 with a standard deviation of 60. Thus, assuming a normal distribution of population size about the mean, two-thirds of all centres would have populations between 181 and 61, i.e., between one standard deviation above and one standard deviation below the mean.

Table 5
Summary Description of Saskatchewan Centres, 1961, 1981 and 1990

Averages of Population and Business Outlets ± One Standard Deviation*

Functional Classification	No. of Centres 1961 1981 1990	1961 Pop.	Bus.	1981 Pop.	Bus.	1990 Pop.	Bus.
Primary Wholesale/Retail	2 2 2	115,582 103,834 92,086	1,649.2 1,525.5 1,401.3	164,345 158,379 152,413	3,758.3 3,438.0 3,117.7	183,488 181,444 179,400	4,508.0 4,213.5 3,929.0
Secondary Wholesale/Retail	8 8 8	23,661 14,160 4,659	399.7 286.8 173.9	27,071 16,713 6,355	754.1 543.8 333.5	28,269 18,088 7,907	764.6 532.6 350.6
Complete Shopping Centre	29 22 6	3,166 2,198 1,230	99.4 77.7 56.0	4,148 3,032 1,916	180.9 133.5 86.1	5,776 4,872 3,968	232.5 196.2 159.9
Partial Shopping Centre	99 30 46	923 659 395	40.6 33.0 25.4	1,814 1,296 778	71.6 56.7 41.8	2,593 1,759 834	95.4 70.0 44.6
Full Convenience Centre	189 136 117	418 296 174	21.2 16.9 12.6	786 541 296	28.3 20.8 13.3	869 575 281	30.8 21.3 11.8
Minimum Convenience Centre	271 400 419	181 121 61	9.2 6.3 3.4	237 125 13	8.0 4.6 1.2	287 141 —	8.6 4.1 —

*The standard deviation is a measure of the amount of variability in the group of centres relative to the average. Two-thirds of the centres within a group will have values for population and business outlets that fall within the range of one standard deviation above and one standard deviation below the respective averages.

Throughout the 1961-90 period, Saskatchewan was going through a process of urbanization. The population of the 598 subject communities was 538,666 in 1961 (approximately 58 percent of the province's total). By 1981 there were 679,622 people living in these centres (approximately 70 percent) and by 1990 the population of these communities was 744,092. With the provincial population at about one million at this time, the subject communities were home to approximately 74 percent of Saskatchewan's people.

The distribution of the population gain was quite uneven however. Between 1961 and 1981 there was a pronounced relative shift to the larger centres. The thirty-two communities in the top three functional categories in 1981 captured 93 percent of the increase experienced by the 598 centres. In terms of number of business outlets, the shift was even more pronounced. The same thirty-two communities gained over 6,500 businesses between 1961 and 1981, while the remainder of the centres lost nearly 1,800. The growth of Saskatoon and Regina was very substantial in absolute terms (as shown in Table 5) and in relative terms as well. The share of the urban system's population accounted for by these two centres rose from 39 percent in 1961 to 47 percent in 1981. Their share of business outlets rose from 19 to 33 percent.

Saskatchewan's business cycle is characterized by wide fluctuations because of the variability in prices received for the basic commodities which form the core of the province's export base. Nevertheless, the period between 1961 and 1981 was characterized by substantial gains. There was a net increase of over 100,000 jobs during these twenty years. Total real personal expenditure on goods and services increased by 210 percent between these same dates. During the years following 1981, gains have been much slower. Net employment had increased from 425,000 to 446,000 by 1989 while real personal expenditure increased by only 18 percent.

Since the provincial economy provides the context within which the urban system evolves, it is useful to keep the performance of Saskatchewan's economy in mind when comparing the experience of the urban system between 1981 and 1990 with the previous period.

The pace of urbanization did not differ that much between the latter and the earlier period. New businesses were created at only about one-third of the previous rate, however. Further, the distribution of the gains differed from the earlier period in that they were concentrated in even fewer communities. The sixteen communities in the top three functional classifications in 1990 captured 94 percent of the population increase realized by the entire urban system between 1981 and 1990 (compared with 93 percent by thirty-two communities between 1961 and 1981). The gain in business outlets was also more concentrated. Regina and Saskatoon gained 1,551 businesses. The eight Secondary Wholesale-Retail centres combined lost eighty-nine. The six centres remaining in the Complete Shopping centre classification gained 133. The remaining 582 communities lost 832 businesses. Regina and Saskatoon continued to increase their share of the totals. Between 1981 and 1990 the proportion of the population of the 598 communities accounted for by these two cities rose from 47 to 49 percent; businesses from 33 to 40 percent.

To summarize the comparison between the earlier and latter periods, urbanization continued at roughly the same pace but provincial economic growth was much slower over the decade of the 1980s than during the previous two decades. Slower provincial growth was accompanied by a much slower pace in the creation of new businesses. The growth in urban population and in new businesses was concentrated in centres in the three top functional classifications in both periods, but between 1981 and 1990 the number of communities in these three categories had fallen from thirty-two to sixteen.

In Table 6 the average number of business outlets, by type, are listed for each functional category for 1990. From this information it is clear that the 419 communities in the Minimum Convenience category no longer provide a meaningful trade-centre function. There is no single function that can be counted on to be present in these places. Full Convenience centres are somewhat better off in that groceries, gasoline, lodging, meals, and financial services are available to consumers. Farm equipment (although perhaps only one brand name), bulk fuel and building materials are available to producers. There are also three to four producers in each of these 117 centres.

Communities in the top four functional classifications do offer most producer and consumer services. Multiple outlets are usually present as well, providing some variety and brand name choice. The majority of the province's producers (83 percent) are also located in the sixty-two places that are included in the top four categories.

Table 6
Average Number of Businesses of Various Types in Saskatchewan Trade Centres – 1990

Type of Business	419 Minimum Convenience	117 Full Convenience	46 Partial Shopping	6 Complete Shopping	8 Secondary Wholesale/ Retail	2 Primary Wholesale/ Retail
All Consumer Serv	2.41	12.42	44.00	123.83	309.25	2057.50
General Store	0.33	0.96	2.50	3.33	5.00	19.50
Grocery Store	0.25	1.20	3.70	6.67	16.50	72.50
Special Food	—	0.37	1.59	4.17	8.25	55.50
Auto Sales	—	0.35	1.80	4.17	10.88	46.50
Gas Station	0.29	1.39	3.57	6.83	19.13	99.00
Clothing Store	—	0.56	3.50	13.33	20.63	147.00
Furniture Store	—	—	0.87	2.50	5.38	42.00
Home Furnishing	—	0.23	1.89	7.50	23.25	142.00
Restaurant	0.16	1.16	3.65	13.00	42.25	342.50
Drug Store	—	0.42	1.52	2.67	6.63	34.50
Special Retail	—	0.44	3.46	12.33	36.75	246.00
Credit Agency	0.27	1.32	3.96	16.17	39.88	388.00
Hotel	0.47	1.40	3.72	8.17	15.88	51.00
Laundries	—	—	0.28	0.83	2.25	22.00
Personal Serv	—	—	0.78	2.33	6.88	46.00
Auto Repair	0.13	0.62	1.98	6.17	20.38	129.00
Car Wash	0.12	0.45	1.63	5.33	17.63	120.50
Recreation	—	0.11	1.02	3.50	5.63	44.00
Bank or C.U.	0.39	1.44	2.59	4.83	6.12	10.00
All Producer Serv	0.62	4.39	12.20	32.83	91.75	1010.00
Warehousing	—	—	0.37	2.50	13.13	79.00
Farm Equipment	0.12	0.92	2.78	5.50	7.88	34.50
Bulk Fuel	0.18	1.28	2.41	4.33	6.88	11.50
Wholesale	0.17	0.68	2.35	8.67	34.75	544.00
Building Materials	0.14	1.36	3.65	7.17	14.25	68.50
Business Services	—	0.15	0.63	4.67	14.88	272.50
All Producers	0.84	4.25	13.78	39.33	131.63	1146.00
Construction	0.48	2.47	7.74	21.50	70.75	641.00
Manufacturing	0.19	0.96	3.59	11.67	33.88	358.00
Transportation	0.17	0.82	2.46	6.17	27.00	147.00
Doctor*	—	87.00	100.00	100.00	100.00	100.00
Hospital*	—	49.00	91.00	100.00	100.00	100.00
Special Health Care*	—	30.00	96.00	100.00	100.00	100.00
High School*	21.00	89.00	98.00	100.00	100.00	100.00
Grain Elevator*	66.00	94.00	98.00	100.00	100.00	50.00

Note: Values less than 0.10 omitted.

* For these variables the percent of communities offering selected facilities is shown.

In Table 7 the sixty-two communities classified into the top four functional categories are listed by name.

Table 7
Saskatchewan Communities in Top Four Functional Categories

Partial Shopping Centre		Complete Shopping Centre	Secondary Wholesale-Retail	Primary Wholesale-Retail
Assiniboia	Lanigan	Humboldt	Estevan	Regina
Balcarres	Macklin	Kindersley	Lloydminster	Saskatoon
Battleford	Maidstone	Meadow Lake	Moose Jaw	
Big River	Maple Creek	Melfort	North Battleford	
Biggar	Melville	Nipawin	Prince Albert	
Canora	Moosomin	Tisdale	Swift Current	
Carlyle	Outlook		Weyburn	
Carnduff	Oxbow		Yorkton	
Cudworth	Preeceville			
Davidson	Raymore			
Esterhazy	Redvers			
Eston	Rosetown			
Foam Lake	Rosthern			
Fort Qu'Appelle	Shaunavon			
Gravelbourg	Shellbrook			
Grenfell	Spiritwood			
Gull Lake	St. Walburg			
Hudson Bay	Unity			
Indian Head	Wadena			
Kamsack	Watrous			
Kelvington	Watson			
Kipling	Whitewood			
Langenburg	Wynyard			

Community Change and Agricultural Income

The viability of communities will be determined in part by the level and stability of the income of the population in the market areas surrounding each centre. In Saskatchewan, the population in the rural areas surrounding these centres is still substantially dependent on agriculture. To approximate the influence of the agricultural industry, data were obtained from Statistics Canada on income variables of Saskatchewan farm families for the twenty crop districts in the province (Statistics Canada, 1991a). The variables for which data for farm families in each of the crop districts were obtained included: a) the average family income of area residents; b) off-farm income relative to total family income; c) aggregate family income in each area; d) aggregate gross sales of agricultural products; e) sales of wheat and other small grains as a percentage of total agricultural sales; and f) livestock sales as a percentage of the total. Variables a, c, and d indicate levels of income while variables b, e, and f are indicators of the degree of on- and off-farm diversification.

Each crop district was compared with the provincial average in order to determine whether the district was better or worse off than the provincial average in terms of each of the six variables. Having higher average income, greater aggregate area income, higher aggregate gross agricultural sales, a larger percentage of total income originating from off-farm employment, and a higher percentage of total agricultural sales originating with livestock were considered positive characteristics. In the case of income originating from off-farm employment and agricultural sales from livestock, percentages above the provincial averages are considered positive indicators. They represent, in the first instance, diversification of the local economy and in the second, diversification on the farm. Diversification is considered a positive attribute of a local economy because it represents an increase in the number and variety of income sources. It can also reduce the variability of income. For the percentage of gross sales originating with wheat and other small grains, a value below the provincial average was considered a positive attribute because it suggests more on-farm diversification.

The income generating characteristics of each crop district, as indicated by the number of positive and negative values, were evaluated in terms of whether the number of positive values outnumbered the negative. Three types of areas were defined:

1. those where positive indicators consistently outnumbered the negative;

2. those where negative indicators outnumbered positive ones consistently; and

3. those areas where the results were mixed.

Type 1 would be considered the crop districts where communities would have a better chance of succeeding. Type 2 would represent the areas with the least attractive environment.

Type 1 includes the eastern and northern crop districts: i.e., districts 1B, 5A, 5B, 6B, 8A, 8B, 9A, 9B. Type 2 includes the southern and western districts: i.e., 2A, 3AS, 3AN, 3BS, 3BN, 4A, 4B, 7A, 7B. Type 3 includes the transition zones between Types 1 and 2 and consists of crop districts 1A, 2B, and 6A. These areas are identified on Figure 2.

In comparing these three areas, the northern area (Type 1) contains 51 percent of the province's communities (302) while the southern contains 32 percent (192). The transition zone (Type 3) contains 104 communities (17 percent of the total).

Table 8
Number of Communities, by Functional Classification,
In Each Economic Area 1961, 1981, and 1990

Economic Area	MCC 61 81 90	FCC 61 81 90	PSC 61 81 90	CSC 61 81 90	SWR 61 81 90	PWR 61 81 90
North	125 190 199	102 77 65	56 15 28	14 15 5	4 4 4	1 1 1
South	102 140 141	51 35 38	24 8 10	13 7 1	2 2 2	– – –
Trans.	44 70 79	36 24 14	19 7 8	2 – –	2 2 2	1 1 1

Throughout the 1961-90 period all but a few of the province's communities experienced decline. Nevertheless, centres in the northern area were less likely to decline than those in the southern area. In Table 8, the number of communities in each functional category are identified for 1961, 1981, and 1990 by the three types of areas. In Table 9, the proportion in each category declining, growing, or remaining stable is shown. Rates of decline in the south consistently exceeded those in the north for all functional categories between 1961 and 1990. For the subperiods, only one instance can be identified in which decline in the north exceeded that in the south. This is for the Full Convenience category between 1981 and 1990.

The division of the province into northern and southern regions roughly follows lines which identify soil zones, vegetation types and moisture regimes. The southern zone is characterized by short-grass prairie, brown soils, as well as lower (and more variable) rainfall. The northern zone includes most of the province's dark brown and black soils, vegetation that ranges from parkland (prairie grasses and isolated stands of mixed hardwoods) to forest. Rainfall is somewhat

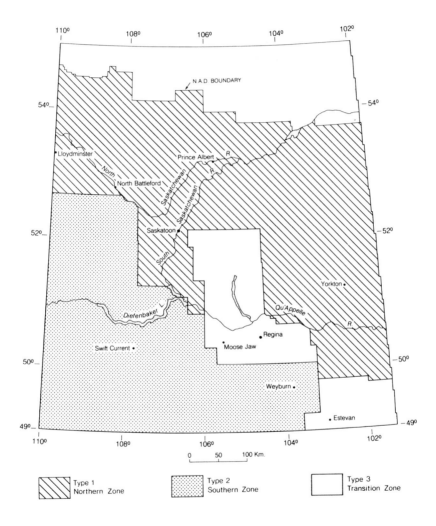

Figure 2. Agricultural Economic Areas in Saskatchewan.

Table 9
Proportion of Communities Declining, Remaining Stable, or Growing by Period

1961-1990

Economic Area	MCC			FCC			PSC			CSC			SWR			PWR		
	D	S	G	D	S	G	D	S	G	D	S	G	D	S	G	D	S	G
North	–	98	2	69	29	2	70	30	–	64	36	–	–	100	–	–	100	–
South	–	100	–	73	27	–	96	4	–	92	8	–	–	100	–	–	–	–
Trans	–	100	–	83	17	–	68	32	–	100	–	–	–	100	–	–	100	–

1961 - 1981

Economic Area	MCC			FCC			PSC			CSC			SWR			PWR		
	D	S	G	D	S	G	D	S	G	D	S	G	D	S	G	D	S	G
North	–	98	2	64	36	–	71	27	2	–	100	–	–	100	–	–	100	–
South	–	100	–	73	27	–	92	8	–	46	54	–	–	100	–	–	–	–
Trans	–	100	–	72	28	–	74	26	–	100	–	–	–	100	–	–	100	–

1981 - 1990

Economic Area	MCC			FCC			PSC			CSC			SWR			PWR		
	D	S	G	D	S	G	D	S	G	D	S	G	D	S	G	D	S	G
North	–	94	6	27	65	8	20	80	–	67	33	–	–	100	–	–	100	–
South	–	97	3	14	83	3	62	38	–	86	14	–	–	100	–	–	–	–
Trans	–	97	3	46	50	4	–	100	–	–	–	–	–	100	–	–	100	–

higher and somewhat less variable (For a complete reference to soil zone characteristics see Mitchell, Moss and Clayton, 1944).

Agricultural development reflects the underlying physical conditions in these regions. The southern zone has been characterized by a higher concentration of wheat and other small-grain crops except in the extreme southwest where range grazing and cow-calf operations are important. The northern zone, on the other hand, has been characterized by a greater diversification of agricultural production. Wheat and other small grains are important in the north but variety has long been provided by oilseeds and forage crops. Livestock is also more important in the northern zone. Farms are smaller and population densities are higher. Changes taking place in grain farming during the past several decades, which have led to the substitution of capital for labour, have had a greater impact on the straight grain-farming activities in the south than on mixed-farming operations in the north.

The presence of activities in addition to agriculture provide opportunities for non-agricultural and off-farm employment. Mining, for example, is important in both the north and the south. Oil and gas exploration and production have benefitted the south more than the north but forestry has been an exclusively northern activity. Tourism, facilitated by the presence of provincial parks, Prince Albert National Park, and other recreational attractions, on balance, favours the north. Developments in the non-agricultural (far-northern) area in Saskatchewan have benefitted suppliers and the service industry based in Saskatoon more than firms based in Regina. Workers from Prince Albert, Saskatoon, Meadow Lake, and Nipawin also benefit from developments in the far north more than workers from communities farther south. Further there is a greater concentration of manufacturing plants in or near communities in the north than in the south. This is facilitated, at least in part, by the higher population densities in the north which provide a larger labour pool from which rural-based manufacturing industries can draw.

Behind the province-wide changes which have affected all of the communities in the provincial trade-centre system lie the improvements in production, transport, and communications technology of the past several decades. These technical changes have had the effect of concentrating numerous, formerly dispersed, activities into fewer and larger urban places. Changes in consumer preferences emphasizing greater variety and quality have, when coupled with improved personal mobility, led to an apparent shift in shopping patterns from local communities to regional centres and the province's major cities. Compared with both the 1941-61 period and the 1961-81 period, the past decade has been characterized by concentration in even fewer centres near the top of the hierarchy. Rural dwellers also appear willing to drive greater distances to shop and work at the beginning of the 1990s than was the case even ten years ago.

If the economic base of each region in Saskatchewan was identical, it is probable that the response of the trade-centre system to changes in technology and shopping patterns would be similar across the province.

Table 10
Number and Percent of High Level Centres in Each Economic Area
1961, 1981, and 1990

A. Top Three Functional Categories						
Economic	1961		1981		1990	
Area	No.	%	No.	%	No.	%
North	19	49	20	63	10	63
South	15	38	9	28	3	19
Trans	5	13	3	9	3	19
	39	100	32	100	16	100
B. Top Four Functional Categories						
Economic	1961		1981		1990	
Area	No.	%	No.	%	No.	%
North	75	54	35	56	38	61
South	39	28	17	27	13	21
Trans	24	17	10	16	11	18
	138	100	62	100	62	100

The variation in the economic base from one region to the next provides a local differential effect to the overall change which can be either positive or negative. This differential is reflected in the data provided in Tables 8 and 9. A further comparison is made in Table 10 which shows the proportion of the province's larger communities situated in each economic area for the three dates used in this analysis. The share of the province's viable communities is shown to increase in the north and decrease in the south based on both the top three and the top four functional categories.

The information provided in Tables 8 through 10 is consistent with the proposition that a more diversified economic base provides a more hospitable environment for community development. The contraction of the trade-centre system has been less rapid in the north throughout the 1961-90 period than in the south.

Has the southern, more grain-dependent region, contracted even more rapidly during the past few years when the small grains industry experienced major difficulties? The data in Tables 8 through 10 do not contradict this proposition. On the other hand, it would be hard to make a strong case for such an hypothesis based only on these data.

In the next section a more micro-level approach is taken to attempt to shed additional light on this question.

Community Level Analysis

Attention has previously been drawn to the decline between 1981 and 1990 of sixteen of the twenty-two communities, which were classified as Complete Shopping centres in 1981. It is interesting to note that all but one of the six centres remaining in the Complete Shopping centre classification are in the northern zone. Four of the six are northeast of Saskatoon: Humboldt, Melfort, Tisdale, and Nipawin, while the fifth, Meadow Lake, is northwest of Saskatoon. The only Complete Shopping centre in the southern area is Kindersley, southwest of Saskatoon about 120 miles. Each of the five centres in the northern zone is situated in local regions that are reasonably well diversified. Oilseeds, forage crops and (a limited amount of other) specialty crops are grown in addition to small grains. Cattle, hogs, and sometimes poultry or bees are also raised. Forest-based activity is important for Meadow Lake and Nipawin. Indian reserves are also situated near to the latter communities which provide a stable base for trade and service outlets. Finally, both have good recreation facilities in their immediate areas.

Kindersley, the only Complete Shopping centre in the southern zone to retain its status, is like most other southern centres in that it serves an agricultural region in which wheat is the major crop produced. Unlike most other southern communities, however, Kindersley is in one of the province's major oil and gas producing areas. Between 20 and 30 percent of Kindersley's labour force is employed in exploration for, or production of, petroleum and natural gas.

The communities which declined from Complete Shopping centre to Partial Shopping centre status between 1981 and 1990 were:

Southern Region   **Northern Region**

Southern Region	Northern Region	
Assiniboia	Biggar	Melville
Fort Qu'Appelle	Canora	Moosomin
Maple Creek	Esterhazy	Outlook
Rosetown	Hudson Bay	Wadena
Shaunavon	Kamsack	Wynyard
Unity		

A study of these communities quickly reveals that their decline in status cannot be attributed solely to differences in the agricultural base in their immediate areas, although this is a contributing factor in several instances. Most of the southern centres which declined do serve primarily a grain economy. Fort Qu'Appelle, however, is a recreation centre as much as an agricultural service centre. What does characterize each of the southern communities, except Fort Qu'Appelle, is a lack of diversification both within the community as well as in the surrounding regions. Another factor which has had an influence on Fort Qu'Appelle, Rosetown, and Unity, however, is their proximity to a much larger community, Regina in the first case, Saskatoon in the second, and North Battleford in the third. By 1990 the pull of the province's cities extended well beyond the forty miles that separate Fort Qu'Appelle and Unity from the larger centre or even the seventy miles that separate Rosetown from Saskatoon. This proximity discourages or precludes the development, or retention, of the higher order functions that distinguish the Complete from the Partial Shopping centres. Note that all of the communities retaining Complete Shopping centre status were not only serving more diversified economies but were separated by substantially greater distances from large centres.

Table 11
Structural Characteristics of Communities that Remained
in Cluster #4 in the 1981 to 1990 Period – 6 Communities

Function	1981 Avg.	Std. Dev.	1990 Avg.	Std. Dev.
Population	4286.67	805.13	4872.33	904.01
All Producers	47.33	7.23	39.33	12.89
Construction	31.00	7.19	21.50	7.32
Manufacturing	10.67	3.09	11.67	3.09
Transportation	5.67	2.49	6.17	4.30
All Producer Serv	27.00	9.71	32.83	6.91
Warehousing	2.17	1.77	2.50	2.06
Farm Equipment	7.17	3.98	5.50	2.63
Bulk Fuel	4.00	2.24	4.33	1.89
Wholesale	5.67	3.82	8.67	2.56
Building Materials	6.83	3.18	7.17	2.11
Business Services	1.17	1.07	4.67	1.60
All Consumer Serv	99.05	18.95	123.83	19.46
General Store	5.00	1.83	3.33	1.25
Grocery Store	7.00	2.58	6.67	1.80
Special Food	3.17	1.21	4.17	2.34
Auto Sales	7.00	2.65	4.17	1.07
Gas Station	7.50	2.14	6.83	3.34
Clothing Store	10.17	3.80	13.33	5.85
Furniture Store	2.00	1.41	2.50	1.12
Home Furnishing	6.17	2.91	7.50	3.10
Restaurant	8.83	2.61	13.00	3.46
Drug Store	3.00	1.29	2.67	1.25
Special Retail	12.00	1.91	12.33	2.49
Credit Agency	1.50	1.71	16.17	7.67
Hotel	5.67	1.25	8.17	2.54
Laundries	1.00	1.41	0.83	0.90
Personal Serv	2.67	0.75	2.33	2.75
Auto Repair	5.83	1.34	6.17	1.77
Car Wash	6.17	2.27	5.33	3.25
Recreation	1.83	0.69	3.50	1.71
Bank or C.U.	3.00	0.58	4.83	1.07

	% present	% present
Doctor	100	100
Hospital	100	100
Special Care	100	100
High School	100	100
Elevator	100	100

Table 12
Structural Characteristics of Communities that Dropped from Cluster #4 to Cluster #3 in the 1981 to 1990 Period – 16 Communities

Function	1981 Avg.	1981 Std. Dev.	1990 Avg.	1990 Std. Dev.
Population	2561.75	761.26	2620.38	789.7
All Producers	25.00	8.22	18.44	5.93
Construction	15.69	4.61	2.92	7.32
Manufacturing	5.69	3.93	5.31	3.01
Transportation	3.63	2.34	2.94	2.05
All Producer Serv	12.69	4.43	15.81	5.09
Warehousing	0.00	0.00	0.50	0.79
Farm Equipment	4.31	2.31	3.56	2.21
Bulk Fuel	2.75	2.17	3.38	1.36
Wholesale	0.44	1.46	3.06	2.63
Building Materials	5.19	2.16	4.56	2.15
Business Services	0.00	0.00	0.75	0.90
All Consumer Serv	57.81	11.74	64.94	14.98
General Store	3.13	1.32	2.88	1.54
Grocery Store	3.94	1.71	4.75	2.30
Special Food	2.81	2.35	2.56	1.90
Auto Sales	3.31	1.72	2.88	1.41
Gas Station	4.75	2.08	5.31	2.93
Clothing Store	5.13	1.54	5.94	2.30
Furniture Store	0.63	0.70	1.00	1.22
Home Furnishing	3.88	2.74	3.06	2.01
Restaurant	5.19	4.07	5.13	2.15
Drug Store	2.06	0.90	2.63	1.45
Special Retail	6.63	2.26	6.50	2.32
Credit Agency	0.75	1.25	6.13	3.48
Hotel	3.63	1.62	5.31	2.36
Laundries	1.25	0.90	0.69	0.68
Personal Serv	1.56	1.17	1.25	0.83
Auto Repair	2.13	1.58	2.56	1.77
Car Wash	4.19	1.98	2.06	1.39
Recreation	0.88	0.70	1.00	0.87
Bank or C.U.	2.00	0.50	3.31	0.92

	% present		% present
Doctor	100		100
Hospital	100		100
Special Care	100		100
High School	100		100
Elevator	100		100

In the northern region, a variety of causes can be found for the decline of the ten communities from Complete Shopping centre status. Hudson Bay was (and is) more dependent on the forest than on agriculture. Recently there has been a major contraction of the forest-based activity in this area due to over-harvesting the resource. Esterhazy grew to its Complete Shopping centre status because of the development of potash mining in the immediate vicinity; but the potash industry has not been buoyant for several years and the level of the mining activity has been reduced. Esterhazy is also constrained in its growth potential as an agricultural service centre because of its proximity to Yorkton. Melville, Canora, and Kamsack are also within thirty to thirty-five miles of Yorkton and thus are limited in the higher order functions that they can develop in competition with the much larger city of Yorkton. Biggar and Outlook are similarly limited by their proximity to Saskatoon.

In Table 11 the structural characteristics of the six communities retaining Complete Shopping centre status are shown for 1981 and 1990. Table 12 provides similar information for the sixteen that declined. A comparison of these tables indicates that the six retaining their status were larger in population in 1981 than those that declined and had a greater number of outlets of nearly all functions as well. The initial advantage of the six that retained their status relative to the sixteen that declined grew over time so that by 1990 the sixteen were more similar to the centres in the tier below (#3) than they were to the six remaining in the Complete Shopping centre category.

In Table 13, the growth of communities in the two groups between 1981 and 1990 is shown in the first two columns by comparing 1990 values for certain characteristics with their 1981 counterparts. An index number in excess of 100.00 indicates positive growth over that time period, while a value of less than 100 reflects decline. The indexes 102.29 and 113.66 indicate, for example, that the population of declining centres grew, on average, by 2.29 percent over the 1980s while the stable communities realized an average population growth of 13.66 percent.

The third column in Table 13 attempts to measure the manner in which communities in the two groups have become less alike. The

Table 13
Comparison of Communities that Retained Complete Shopping Centre Status Between 1981 and 1990 with Those that Declined to Partial Shopping Centre Status

Function	1990 Indexes for Centres		Index of Relative Change[1]
	Declining	Stable	
Population	102.29	113.66	111.12
All Producers	73.76	83.10	112.66
Transportation	80.99	108.82	134.36
Manufacturing	93.32	109.37	117.20
Construction	64.95	69.35	106.77
All Producer Services	124.59	121.59	97.59
Business Services	—[2]	399.15	622.67[3]
Warehousing	—[2]	115.21	500.00[3]
Building Materials	87.86	104.98	119.49
Farm Equipment	81.44	76.71	94.19
Bulk Fuel	122.91	108.25	88.07
Wholesale	695.45	152.91	21.99
All Consumer Services	112.33	124.45	110.79
Car Wash	49.16	86.39	175.73
Recreation Services	113.64	191.26	168.30
Home Furnishings	78.87	121.56	154.13
Laundries	55.20	83.00	150.36
Restaurant	98.84	147.23	148.96
Special Food	91.10	131.55	144.40
Credit Agency	817.33	1078.00	131.89
Clothing Store	115.79	131.07	113.20
Personal Services	80.13	87.27	108.91
Special Retail	98.04	102.75	104.80
Hotel	146.28	144.09	98.50
Bank or CU	165.50	161.00	97.28
Auto Repair	120.19	105.83	88.05
Gas Station	111.79	91.07	81.47
Grocery Store	120.56	95.29	79.04
Furniture Store	158.73	125.00	78.75
General Store	92.01	66.60	72.38
Drug Store	127.67	89.00	69.71

[1]The index of relative change is calculated as the 1990 index of stable centres divided by the 1990 index of declining centres. For example, for population, 113.66 ÷ 102.29 = 111.12.

[2]Fewer than 0.10 outlets per centre in 1981.

[3]1990 index for stable communities divided by 1990 index for declining communities.

entries in this column are obtained by dividing the 1990 index for stable communities by the 1990 index for declining communities. An example is provided in footnote 1 to Table 13. To elaborate on this example, the six stable communities had an index of population relative to the sixteen that declined of 167.33 in 1981, i.e., population size was initially 67 percent higher. By 1990, this index had risen to 185.94, showing average population size now 86 percent higher. This represents a gain in the index for the stable communities relative to the declining ones over this period of 11.12 percent, i.e., the value of the index is $111.12 = 185.94 \div 167.33$.

Index numbers in excess of 100.00 identify those functions in which the six stable communities gained relative to the sixteen that declined, and thus the activities in which they became less alike. The producer functions in which the six centres grew relative to the sixteen centres that declined were transportation, manufacturing and (marginally) construction. Of producer services, business services expanded substantially in the six, but only very marginally in the sixteen, reflecting the growth in diversified producer activities served from the six stable communities. Warehousing and building materials also grew more rapidly in the six.

In terms of consumer services, the six distinguished themselves from the sixteen by the development of a range of convenience and specialty functions again indicative of a more diversified base which provides a more steady stream of consumer income. It is probably the case that there is more off-farm employment and more two-income families in the areas served by the six stable communities.

Index numbers less than 100.00 identify those activities in which the sixteen gained relative to the six. Thus, in services to the agricultural industry and in the provision of everyday consumer services, the sixteen gained relative to the six. This could have occurred either because growth was faster for these functions in the sixteen than in the six or because decline was faster in the six. Examples of both types can be found in comparing the first two columns of Table 13. Note that in all cases, however, the six stable communities still have more outlets of all functions than the sixteen. The sixteen, in effect, have retained their agricultural service and routine consumer service functions and, relative to the six stable communities, have come to depend even more upon them than previously. The six have retained these functions, as well, but have developed new ones which they have come to depend on relatively more than previously.

In summary to this section it is clear that over the 1961-90 period, communities in the south have not fared as well as those in the north. During the 1981-90 period, communities primarily dependent on the grain economy have probably fared worse than those serving more diversified local economies. Northern communities have, on average, done better because the north offers greater potential for on-farm diversification and is characterized by greater off-farm diversity as well.

When it gets down to particular cases, several other influences are seen to be important, especially initial size and proximity to a larger centre.

Trade Centre Change and Access to Agricultural Inputs

The preceding discussion would probably lead one to conclude that access to agricultural inputs may have become difficult, involving much more time than previously, and necessitating many more miles of travel. It certainly has been the case that, between 1961 and 1990, equipment dealers and farm-service outlets have shifted from Minimum Convenience to Full Convenience and Partial Shopping centres. Consequently, it is the case that, on average, the producer must travel somewhat farther to obtain replacement parts or supplies or to buy a new implement.

What must be considered, however, is the large number of centres that Saskatchewan had at the beginning of the adjustment period. Compared with Manitoba, which in 1961 had 219 communities ranging between fifty and 999 in population, and Alberta which had 259, Saskatchewan's 549 communities in this size range was greater than the sum of the other two prairie provinces combined. Communities in Saskatchewan were, in fact, about ten miles apart. Since 1961 the number of centres providing a viable trade-centre role has declined substantially; but access has improved dramatically as well, as previously noted.

As an initial approximation of the market areas of Partial Shopping and higher order centres, circles of thirty-five mile radius were drawn on a provincial highway map around the sixty-two centres in the four top functional categories. On this map, every circle overlapped with more than one other circle. All of these communities provide multiple implement, bulk fuel, and farm supply outlets. In most places, producers would have the option of several centres within a twenty-mile drive. It is hard to find a location, outside the far south and far southwest which is even thirty-five miles from one of these sixty-two communities. The areas not included within a circle in the south and southwest include the Great Sand Hills, the Vermilion Hills, and other sparsely inhabited areas devoted largely to cattle ranching.

In addition to these sixty-two communities, there are 117 additional Full Convenience centres which do provide some minimal level of support to producers as well as consumers. If circles were drawn around these 119 additional centres, virtually the entire area of the map would be enclosed and most would be overlapped with several circles.

To put these thirty-five mile-radius circles into a context, 1981 Statistics Canada data indicate that rural dwellers presently drive an average of about thirty-five miles one-way to work (Statistics Canada, 1991b). It may be concluded, therefore, that while the travelling distance required to obtain farm supplies has increased during the adjustment period, these distances are not unduly burdensome or unrealistic. It is also abundantly clear that the provincial economy is incapable of supporting a greater number of centres.

A final perspective on trade-centre change is provided by comparing Figures 3, 4, and 5 on which the spatial arrangement of trade centres is shown for 1961, 1981 and 1990. Communities in the four top functional classifications (the black symbols) are clearly less numerous in 1990 than in 1961 (62 versus 140). Spacing is also more systematic in that there are fewer adjacent pairs of similar status today than thirty years ago.

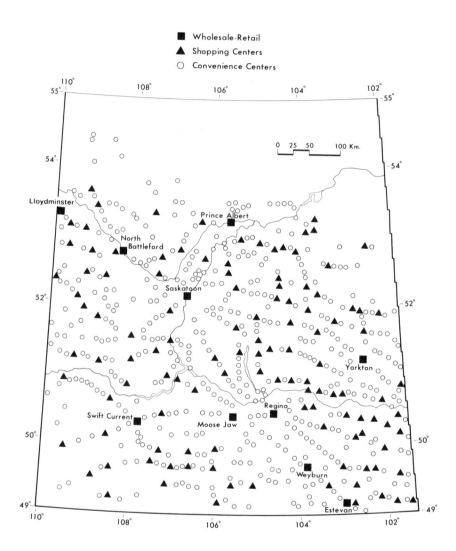

Figure 3. Saskatchewan Trade Centres by Functional Hierarchy, 1961.

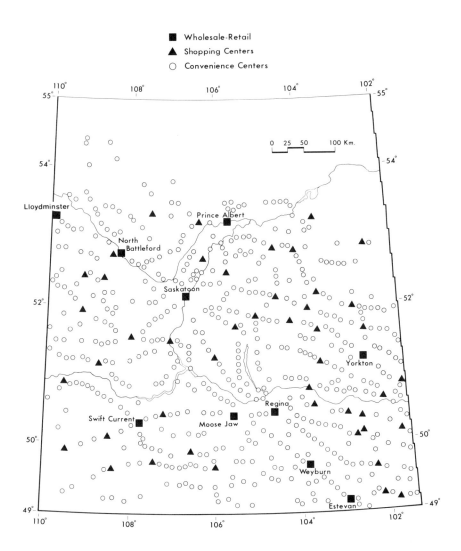

Figure 4. Saskatchewan Trade Centres by Functional Hierarchy, 1981.

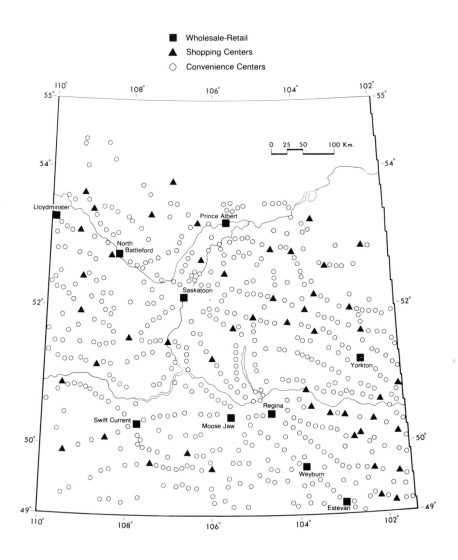

Figure 5. Saskatchewan Trade Centres by Functional Hierarchy, 1990.

6

Conclusions

The Past

The concentration of Saskatchewan's population and businesses in the province's larger centres, accompanied by stagnation or decline of small communities, began in the early 1940s and has continued through to the present.

Between 1941 and 1961 many communities of intermediate size gained population and business outlets as did the largest centres. During the 1960s, 1970s and 1980s, however, the concentration of population and economic activity has been increasingly in the province's largest communities. In the twenty years between 1961 and 1981, for example, the thirty-two largest centres captured 93 percent of the population growth realized by the entire system of communities. Between 1981 and 1990, the gains were even more concentrated — the sixteen largest communities accounted for 94 percent of the population growth. In terms of business outlets the largest thirty-two centres gained 6,500 business outlets between 1961 and 1981 while the remaining 566 places lost 1800. During the 1980s nearly all of the net gain in business outlets was realized by Saskatoon and Regina.

Most of the consolidation and concentration of the past fifty years can be attributed to changes in technology in agricultural and other primary activities, as well as in the transportation, communications and distribution industries.

Provincial and federal government policies have also contributed to the reorganization and concentration of activity in fewer, larger, centrally located places. Government departments, organized along functional lines, pursue objectives within their functional mandates. Schools and hospitals have closed in rural areas and small centres in order to provide larger facilities and a wider range of services in larger, regionally central, communities, and in response to a declining local population base. Post offices, grain elevators, and numerous other activities have followed a similar course. Shopping patterns of rural dwellers have also altered becoming much like those of their urban counterparts. Rural people now routinely shop in distant communities where greater variety and lower prices are available.

The migration of people and economic activity into the cities has continued through good times and bad. The stage of the business cycle may have affected the pace of consolidation but not the pattern. Rural and small community decline clearly cannot be attributed solely, or even primarily, to the depressed grain markets of recent years. Indeed, an improvement in agricultural prices may accelerate, rather than slow, the pace of consolidation in some areas.

Geographically, the economic base of the region served by a community does influence its viability. Centres in southern and southwestern Saskatchewan experienced faster rates of decline than communities in the more northern regions of the province. Southern communities serve an agricultural economy which is dominated by cattle ranching and the production of small grains. Land quality and productivity have dictated increasing farm size and thus fewer farm families. Agriculture in the northern region of the province is more diversified and farms are smaller. Livestock, oilseeds, and specialty crops provide some alternative to specialization in grains. Diversification into forestry-based activity and tourism also favours the north. Higher population densities permit greater diversification of income sources and employment opportunities within these northern communities than in the south. Manufacturing and specialized business services, for example, have contributed to the stability or growth of several northern communities and their surrounding populations.

The Future

To observe the patterns of consolidation of the past fifty years raises questions about what the future holds for Saskatchewan's rural communities. For many, the process is irreversible. Population decline, coupled with the loss of infrastructure and commercial outlets, has gone beyond the point where an increase in agricultural (or other) income would reverse their fortunes. Such communities typically lie within the market area of a larger centre. Investors, private and public, attempt to build on existing strengths rather than deliberately oppose established trends. Thus several hundred of Saskatchewan's smallest places appear destined to eventually disappear, though the process may be spread over many years. As long as the remaining businesses are able to recover operating costs, and a little more, and as long as the existing housing stock provides adequate shelter, a few people will continue to live in these communities.

At the upper end of the hierarchy survival is not a question. It is not a matter of whether the largest communities will continue to exist but, rather, how well they will do.

Shopping patterns, as we understand them at this time, seem to suggest evolution toward a system characterized by three types of centres (rather than the historically observed six). These are cities, regional shopping centres and convenience centres. Saskatoon, Regina, and the next eight largest communities will undoubtably continue to function as major providers of consumer goods and services. The two largest cities will provide high-level business, medical, educational, transportation and wholesale services to the entire province. The next eight largest communities will provide these same functions to their respective areas of the province.

The second tier of centres consists of the combination of the Complete and Partial Shopping centres, fifty-two communities in total, which serve a regional trade-centre function. They provide everyday consumer and producers goods, along with routine educational, government and professional services to areas of between 3,500 and 4,000 square miles. These communities play a very important role in the rural economy. In addition to offering the common goods and services required for everyday life, these centres provide approximately three-quarters of the non-farm jobs available in rural Saskatchewan. The complete range of goods and services that support the agriculture industry are also found in these centres.

A third tier includes the 117 Full Convenience centres and some of the larger, better-located Minimum Convenience centres. These communities house a few common retail outlets typically offering groceries, gasoline, lodging, meals and banking. A few producer services are also commonly available including bulk fuels, building materials, equipment parts, fertilizer and chemicals. The role of these communities is much like that of the 7-Eleven stores found in most urban neighbourhoods except that, in the rural setting, a minimal set of producer services is provided in addition to the conventional consumer services.

The majority of the 419 Minimum Convenience centres have no systematic role in today's trade-centre system although some may offer an isolated, locally important service for a while. Only through an unlikely fortuitous event will any of these communities regain a functional position in the trade-centre system.

What the urban hierarchy will look like in the future depends upon the rate of rural depopulation and upon public and private investment decisions. The present rural population is sufficient to support the majority of the communities which currently provide a rural 7-Eleven type service. Further depopulation or subdivisions of their market areas, on the other hand, would cause these places to lose their remaining trade-centre functions, becoming like the smallest class of today's communities.

At the opposite extreme, the future of the province's cities, performing their present functions, is virtually assured.

It is the fifty-two regional shopping centres that can be most affected by private and public investment decisions at this stage of the process. Much public and private infrastructure will be consolidated in rural Saskatchewan during the 1990s and some new facilities will be constructed. In the past such decisions have usually been made without regard to the impact that the decision would have on the functional relationships among the regional constellation of centres.

In the future, for example, hospitals and schools will be provided in fewer locations. Rail branch lines will be abandoned, numerous country elevators closed, and a few large inland terminals will be constructed. If both the consolidation and the new construction are undertaken with a view to strengthening the present fifty-two Complete and Partial Shopping centres, they can continue to perform the very important functions they now provide to residents of rural Saskatchewan. Such an approach would represent a distinct break with past practice. Provincial governments in particular will have to avoid the narrow political interests which have all too frequently been the basis for allocating public investment in the past. Selectivity based upon recognition of the contribution that regional concentration of public infrastructure can have on maintaining the viability of the system of rural trade centres must become the guiding criterion. Private companies, too, should systematically consider the impact that their actions will have on the regional constellation of communities in addition to the corporate interests of the firm.

Appendix

List of Names of All Communities Included in the Study and their 1961, 1981, and 1990 Status in the Trade-Centre Hierarchy

Community	1961 Cluster	1981 Cluster	1990 Cluster
Abbey	2	2	1
Aberdeen	2	2	1
Abernethy	1	1	2
Adanac	1	1	1
Admiral	1	1	1
Alameda	2	1	1
Albertville	1	1	1
Algrove	1	1	1
Alida	2	1	1
Allan	2	2	2
Alsask	1	1	1
Alvena	2	1	1
Amsterdam	1	1	1
Aneroid	2	1	1
Annaheim	n/a	n/a	1
Antler	2	1	1
Arborfield	3	2	2
Archerville	2	1	2
Arcola	3	2	1
Ardath	1	1	1
Ardill	1	1	1
Arelee	1	1	1
Arran	2	1	1
Asquith	2	1	1
Assiniboia	4	4	3
Atwater	1	1	1
Avonlea	2	2	2
Aylesbury	2	1	1
Aylsham	2	1	1
Balcarres	3	2	3
Baldwinton	1	1	1
Balgonie	2	2	1
Bangor	1	1	1

1 = Minimum Convenience; 2 = Full Convenience; 3 = Partial Shopping Centre;
4 = Complete Shopping Centre; 5 = Secondary Wholesale-Retail; 6 = Primary
Wholesale-Retail.

Community	1961 Cluster	1981 Cluster	1990 Cluster
Bankend	1	1	1
Battleford	3	3	3
Beatty	1	1	1
Beaubier	1	1	1
Beechy	2	2	2
Belle Plaine	1	1	1
Bellegarde	1	1	1
Bengough	3	2	2
Benson	1	1	1
Bertwell	1	1	1
Bethune	2	1	2
Beverley	1	1	1
Bienfait	3	2	1
Big Beaver	1	1	1
Big River	2	2	3
Biggar	4	4	3
Birch Hills	3	2	2
Birsay	1	1	1
Bjorkdale	n/a	n/a	1
Bladworth	1	1	1
Blaine Lake	3	2	2
Blumenheim	1	1	1
Blumenhof	1	1	1
Blumenort	1	1	1
Blumenthal	1	1	1
Borden	2	2	2
Bounty	1	1	1
Bracken	1	1	1
Bradwell	1	1	1
Brancepath	1	1	1
Bredenbury	2	1	2
Briercrest	2	1	1
Broadview	3	3	2
Brock	2	1	1
Broderick	1	1	1
Brownlee	1	1	1
Bruno	3	2	2
Buchanan	2	1	2
Bulyea	n/a	n/a	1
Burstall	2	2	2
Cabri	3	2	2
Cadillac	2	1	1
Calder	2	1	1
Candiac	1	1	1
Canora	4	4	3

Community	1961 Cluster	1981 Cluster	1990 Cluster
Canwood	2	2	2
Carievale	2	1	1
Carlton	1	1	1
Carlyle	3	3	3
Carmel	1	1	1
Carnduff	3	3	3
Caron	1	1	1
Carragana	2	1	1
Carrot River	3	3	2
Cedoux	1	1	1
Central Butte	3	2	2
Ceylon	2	1	1
Chamberlain	2	1	1
Chaplin	2	1	1
Chelan	1	1	1
Chitek Lake	1	1	1
Choiceland	2	2	2
Chortitz	1	1	1
Churchbridge	2	2	2
Clair	1	1	1
Claybank	1	1	1
Climax	3	2	2
Cochin	1	1	1
Coderre	2	1	1
Codette	1	2	1
Coleville	2	1	2
Colgate	1	1	1
Collacott Subd.	1	1	1
Colonsay	2	2	2
Congress	1	1	1
Conquest	2	1	1
Consul	2	1	1
Corning	1	1	1
Coronach	2	2	2
Courval	1	1	1
Craik	3	2	2
Crane Valley	1	1	1
Craven	1	1	1
Creelman	2	1	2
Crooked River	1	1	1
Crutwell	1	1	1
Crystal Springs	1	1	1
Cudworth	3	3	3
Cupar	3	2	2
Cutknife	3	2	2

Community	1961 Cluster	1981 Cluster	1990 Cluster
Dafoe	1	1	1
Dalmeny	2	2	2
Danbury	1	1	1
D'Arcy	1	1	1
Davidson	3	3	3
Davin	1	1	1
Debden	2	2	2
Delisle	3	2	2
Delmas	1	1	1
Demaine	1	1	1
Denholm	1	1	1
Denzil	2	1	1
Dilke	1	1	1
Dinsmore	3	2	2
Disley	1	1	1
Dodsland	3	2	2
Dollard	1	1	1
Domremy	2	2	1
Dorintosh	1	1	1
Drake	2	1	1
Drinkwater	1	1	1
Dubuc	2	1	1
Duck Lake	2	2	2
Duff	2	1	1
Dunblane	1	1	1
Dundurn	2	1	1
Duval	2	1	1
Dysart	2	1	2
Earl Grey	2	1	1
Eastend	3	2	2
Eatonia	3	2	2
Ebenezer	1	1	1
Edam	2	2	2
Edenwold	2	1	1
Edgeley	1	1	1
Elbow	2	1	1
Elfros	1	1	1
Elrose	3	2	2
Elstow	2	1	1
Endeavor	1	1	1
Englefield	1	2	1
Ernfold	1	1	1
Erwood	1	1	1
Esk	1	1	1
Esterhazy	4	4	3

Community	1961 Cluster	1981 Cluster	1990 Cluster
Estevan	5	5	5
Eston	4	3	3
Evesham	1	1	1
Eyebrow	2	1	1
Fairholme	1	1	1
Fairlight	2	1	1
Fairy Glen	1	1	1
Fenwood	1	1	1
Ferland	n/a	n/a	n/a
Fielding	1	1	1
Fife Lake	2	1	1
Fillmore	2	2	2
Findlater	1	1	1
Fir Mountain	1	1	1
Fiske	1	1	1
Flaxcombe	1	1	1
Fleming	2	1	1
Foam Lake	3	3	3
Forgan	1	1	1
Forget	1	1	1
Fort Qu'Appelle	4	4	3
Fox Valley	2	2	2
Francis	2	1	1
Frenchman Butte	1	1	1
Frobisher	2	1	1
Frontier	2	2	2
Fulda	1	1	1
Furdale	1	1	1
Gainsborough	3	2	2
Garrick	1	1	1
Gerald	1	1	1
Girvin	1	1	1
Glaslyn	2	2	2
Glen Ewen	2	1	1
Glenavon	2	2	1
Glenbain	1	1	1
Glenbush	1	1	1
Glenside	1	1	1
Glentworth	2	1	1
Glidden	1	1	1
Golden Prairie	2	1	1
Goodeve	2	1	1
Goodsoil	2	2	1
Goodwater	1	1	1
Gorlitz	1	1	1

Community	1961 Cluster	1981 Cluster	1990 Cluster
Govan	3	2	1
Grand Coulee	1	1	1
Gravelbourg	4	3	3
Gray	1	1	1
Grayson	2	1	1
Greenfeld	1	1	1
Grenfell	3	3	3
Griffin	1	1	1
Gronlid	1	1	1
Gruenthal	1	1	1
Guernsey	1	1	1
Gull Lake	4	3	3
Hafford	3	2	2
Hagen	1	1	1
Hague	2	2	2
Halbrite	1	1	1
Handel	1	1	1
Hanley	2	2	2
Hardy	1	1	1
Harris	2	2	1
Hawarden	2	1	1
Hazel Dell	1	1	1
Hazenmore	1	1	1
Hazlet	n/a	n/a	1
Hendon	1	1	1
Henribourg	1	1	1
Hepburn	2	2	1
Herbert	3	3	2
Herschel	1	1	1
Heward	1	1	1
Hitchcock	1	1	1
Hodgeville	2	2	2
Hoey	1	1	1
Holdfast	2	1	1
Hubbard	2	1	1
Hudson Bay	3	4	3
Humboldt	4	4	4
Hyas	2	1	1
Imperial	3	2	2
Indian Head	4	3	3
Insinger	1	1	1
Invermay	3	2	2
Ituna	3	3	2
Jansen	2	1	1
Jasmin	1	1	1

Community	1961 Cluster	1981 Cluster	1990 Cluster
Jedburgh	2	1	1
Kamsack	4	4	3
Kayville	1	1	1
Keeler	1	1	1
Kelfield	1	1	1
Kelliher	2	2	1
Kelvington	3	3	3
Kenaston	2	2	2
Kendal	1	1	1
Kennedy	2	1	1
Kenosee Lake	1	1	1
Kerrobert	4	3	2
Khedive	1	1	1
Killaly	2	1	2
Kincaid	3	2	1
Kindersley	4	4	4
Kinistino	3	2	2
Kinley	1	1	1
Kipling	3	3	3
Kisbey	2	1	1
Kronau	1	1	1
Krydor	2	1	1
Kurocki	1	1	1
Kyle	3	2	2
Lac Vert	1	1	1
Lacadena	1	1	1
Lafleche	3	2	2
Laird	1	1	1
Lajord	1	1	1
Lake Alma	2	1	1
Lake Lenore	2	2	1
Lampman	3	2	2
Lancer	1	1	1
Landis	2	2	1
Lang	2	1	1
Langbank	1	1	1
Langenburg	3	3	3
Langham	2	2	2
Lanigan	3	3	3
Lamport	1	1	1
Lashburn	3	2	2
Laura	1	1	1
Lawson	1	1	1
Leader	4	3	2
Leask	2	2	2

Community	1961 Cluster	1981 Cluster	1990 Cluster
Leipzig	1	1	1
Lemburg	3	2	1
Lemsford	1	1	1
Leoville	2	2	2
Leross	2	1	1
Leroy	2	1	2
Leslie	1	1	1
Lestock	2	2	1
Liberty	2	1	1
Limerick	2	1	1
Lintlaw	2	1	1
Lipton	3	2	1
Lisieux	1	1	1
Livelong	1	1	2
Lloydminster	5	5	5
Lockwood	1	1	1
Lone Rock	1	1	1
Loon Lake	2	2	2
Loreburn	2	2	1
Lorlie	1	1	1
Love	1	1	1
Loverna	1	1	1
Lucky Lake	3	2	2
Lumsden	2	2	2
Luseland	3	2	2
Macdowall	1	1	1
Macklin	3	2	3
MacNutt	2	1	1
Macoun	1	1	1
Macrorie	1	1	1
Madison	1	1	1
Maidstone	3	2	3
Major	2	1	1
Manitou Beach	1	1	1
Mankota	3	2	2
Manor	2	2	1
Mantario	1	1	1
Maple Creek	4	4	3
Marcelin	2	1	1
Marchwell	1	1	1
Marengo	1	1	1
Margo	2	1	1
Markinch	1	1	1
Marquis	1	1	1
Marsden	2	2	1

Community	1961 Cluster	1981 Cluster	1990 Cluster
Marshall	1	1	1
Maryfield	3	2	2
Mayfair	1	1	1
Maymont	2	1	1
Mazenod	2	1	1
McCord	1	1	1
McKague	1	1	1
McTaggart	1	1	1
Meacham	2	1	1
Meadow Lake	4	4	4
Meath Park	2	1	2
Medstead	2	1	1
Melaval	1	1	1
Melfort	4	4	4
Melville	4	4	3
Mendham	2	1	1
Meota	1	1	1
Mervin	2	1	1
Meskanaw	1	1	1
Meyronne	1	1	1
Midale	3	2	2
Middle Lake	n/a	n/a	1
Mikado	1	1	1
Milden	3	2	2
Milestone	2	2	2
Minton	n/a	n/a	1
Montmartre	3	2	2
Moose Jaw	5	5	5
Moosomin	4	4	3
Morse	2	2	1
Mortlach	1	1	1
Mossbank	3	2	2
Mozart	1	1	1
Muenster	2	1	1
Naicam	3	2	2
Neidpath	1	1	1
Neilburg	3	2	2
Netherhill	1	1	1
Neuanlage	1	1	1
Neudorf	3	1	1
Neuhorst	1	1	1
Neville	2	1	1
Nipawin	4	4	4
Nokomis	3	2	2
Norquay	3	2	2

Community	1961 Cluster	1981 Cluster	1990 Cluster
North Battleford	5	5	5
North Portal	1	1	1
Northside	1	1	1
Nut Mountain	1	1	1
Odessa	2	1	1
Ogema	2	2	2
Ormiston	1	1	1
Osage	1	1	1
Oungre	1	1	1
Outlook	4	4	3
Oxbow	3	3	3
Paddockwood	2	1	1
Palmer	1	1	1
Pambrun	1	1	1
Pangman	2	2	2
Paradise Hill	2	2	2
Parkbeg	1	1	1
Parkerview	1	1	1
Parkside	1	1	1
Parry	1	1	1
Pathlow	1	1	1
Paynton	1	1	1
Peerless	1	1	1
Pelly	2	2	1
Pennant	2	1	1
Pense	1	1	1
Penzance	1	1	1
Perdue	2	2	2
Perigord	1	1	1
Peterson	1	1	1
Piapot	2	1	1
Pierceland	n/a	n/a	2
Plato	1	1	1
Pleasant Heights	1	1	1
Pleasantdale	1	1	1
Plenty	2	2	1
Plunkett	1	1	1
Ponteix	3	3	2
Porcupine Plain	3	2	2
Portreeve	1	1	1
Prairie River	1	1	1
Preeceville	3	3	3
Prelate	2	1	1
Primate	1	1	1
Prince Albert	5	5	5

Community	1961 Cluster	1981 Cluster	1990 Cluster
Prud'homme	2	2	1
Punnichy	3	2	2
Quill Lake	3	2	1
Quinton	2	1	1
Qu'Appelle	3	2	1
Rabbit Lake	2	2	2
Radisson	3	2	2
Radville	3	2	2
Rama	2	1	1
Raymore	2	2	3
Red Wing Terrace	1	1	1
Redvers	3	2	3
Regina	6	6	6
Regina Beach	2	2	1
Reward	1	1	1
Rhein	2	1	1
Rheinland	1	1	1
Rhineland	1	1	1
Riceton	1	1	1
Richard	1	1	1
Richlea	1	1	1
Richmound	2	1	2
Ridgedale	2	1	1
Riverhurst	3	1	1
Riverside	1	1	1
Robsart	1	1	1
Rocanville	3	2	2
Roche Percee	1	1	1
Rockglen	3	2	2
Rockhaven	1	1	1
Rose Valley	3	2	2
Rosenhof	1	1	1
Rosetown	4	4	3
Rosthern	3	3	3
Rouleau	2	2	1
Ruddell	1	1	1
Runnymede	1	1	1
Rush Lake	1	1	1
Ruthilda	1	1	1
Saltcoats	2	1	1
Salvador	1	1	1
Saskatoon	6	6	6
Sceptre	2	1	1
Schoenfeld	1	1	1
Scott	1	1	1

Community	1961 Cluster	1981 Cluster	1990 Cluster
Scout Lake	1	1	1
Sedley	1	1	1
Semans	3	2	1
Senlac	2	1	1
Shackelton	1	1	1
Shamrock	2	1	1
Shaunavon	4	4	3
Sheho	2	1	1
Shell Lake	2	1	1
Shellbrook	3	3	3
Silton	1	1	1
Simmie	1	1	1
Simpson	2	1	1
Sintaluta	n/a	n/a	1
Smeaton	2	1	2
Smiley	2	1	1
Snowden	1	1	1
Somme	1	1	1
Sonningdale	1	1	1
Southey	3	2	2
Sovereign	1	1	1
Spalding	3	1	2
Speers	2	1	1
Spiritwood	3	3	3
Springfield	1	1	1
Spring Valley	1	1	1
Springside	2	1	1
Springwater	1	1	1
Spruce Lake	1	1	1
Spy Hill	2	1	1
Stalwart	1	1	1
Star City	3	2	1
Stenen	2	1	1
Stewart Valley	2	1	1
Stockholm	2	1	1
Stornoway	1	1	1
Storthoaks	1	1	1
Stoughton	3	2	2
Stranraer	1	1	1
Strasbourg	3	2	2
Strongfield	2	1	1
Sturgis	3	2	2
St. Benedict	n/a	n/a	1
St. Brieux	2	1	1
St. Front	1	1	1

Community	1961 Cluster	1981 Cluster	1990 Cluster
St. Gregor	2	1	2
St. Isadore de Bellevue	n/a	n/a	n/a
St. Louis	2	1	1
St. Walburg	3	2	3
Success	1	1	1
Summerberry	1	1	1
Swift Current	5	5	5
Sylvania	1	1	1
Tadmore	1	1	1
Tantallon	2	1	1
Tessier	1	1	1
Theodore	2	2	2
Tisdale	4	4	4
Togo	2	1	1
Tompkins	2	1	1
Torquay	2	1	1
Tramping Lake	2	1	1
Tribune	1	1	1
Trossachs	1	1	1
Tuffnell	1	1	1
Tugaske	2	1	1
Turtleford	3	2	2
Tuxford	1	1	1
Tway	1	1	1
Tyner	1	1	1
Tyvan	1	1	1
Unity	4	4	3
Val Marie	2	1	1
Valparaiso	1	1	1
Vanguard	3	2	2
Vanscoy	1	1	1
Vawn	1	1	1
Venn	1	1	1
Veregin	2	1	1
Verwood	1	1	1
Vibank	2	2	1
Viceroy	2	1	1
Victoire	1	1	1
Viscount	2	2	1
Vonda	2	2	2
Wadena	4	4	3
Wakaw	3	2	2
Waldeck	1	1	1
Waldheim	2	2	2
Waldron	1	1	1

Community	1961 Cluster	1981 Cluster	1990 Cluster
Wapella	3	2	2
Warman	n/a	n/a	3
Waseca	1	1	1
Watrous	4	3	3
Watson	3	3	3
Wawota	3	2	2
Webb	1	1	1
Weekes	2	1	1
Weirdale	1	1	1
Weldon	2	1	1
Welwyn	2	1	1
West Bend	1	1	1
Weyburn	5	5	5
White Bear	1	1	1
White Fox	2	1	1
Whitewood	3	2	3
Wilcox	1	1	1
Wilkie	4	3	2
Willmar	1	1	1
Willowbrook	1	1	1
Willow Bunch	3	2	2
Windthorst	2	2	1
Wiseton	2	1	1
Wishart	2	1	2
Wolseley	3	2	2
Wood Mountain	2	1	1
Woodrow	1	1	1
Wroxton	1	1	1
Wymark	1	1	1
Wynyard	4	4	3
Yellow Creek	2	1	1
Yellowgrass	2	1	1
Yorkton	5	5	5
Young	2	1	1
Zealandia	1	1	1
Zelma	1	1	1
Zenon Park	3	2	1

References

Allen, P.M. and M. Sanglier. 1979. "A Dynamic Model of Growth in a Central Place System." *Geographical Analysis* 11: 256-72.

———. 1981. "Urban Evolution, Self Organization and Decisionmaking." *Environment and Planning A* 13: 167-83.

———. 1982. "A Dynamic Model of a Central Place System — II." *Geographical Analysis* 13: 149-64.

Anderson, A.H. 1950. "Space as a Social Cost." *Journal of Farm Economics* 32: 411-30.

———. 1953. The Changing Role of the Small Town in Farm Areas. Nebraska AES Special Bulletin 419. Lincoln.

———. 1961. The Expanding Rural Community. Nebraska AES Special Bulletin 464. Lincoln.

Barger, Harold and Hans Landsberg. 1942. *American Agriculture, 1899-1939: A Study of Output, Employment and Productivity.* New York: National Bureau of Economic Research.

Beckmann, Martin J. 1958. "City Hierarchies and the Distribution of City Size." *Economic Development and Cultural Change* 6: 243-48.

———. 1968. *Location Theory.* New York: Random House.

Beckmann, Martin J. and J.C. McPherson. 1970. "City Size Distribution in a Central Place Hierarchy: An Alternative Approach." *Journal of Regional Science* 10: 25-33.

Beguin, Hubert. 1979, "Urban Hierarchy and the Rank-Size Distribution." *Geographical Analysis* 11:149-64.

———. 1982. "City Size Distribution and Central Place Models: A Suggestion." *Journal of Regional Science* 22: 225-39.

———. 1983. "City Size Distributions, Consumption Structure, and Labour Productivity: Modeling and Simulation Results." *Geographical Analysis* 15: 156-63.

Berry, Brian J.L. 1973. *Growth Centres in the American Urban System.* Cambridge, MA: Ballinger.

Berry, B.J.L. et al. 1988. *Market Centres and Retail Location: Theory and Applications.* Englewood Cliffs, Prentice-Hall.

Borchert, John R. and Russell B. Adams. 1963. *Trade Centres and Tributary Areas of the Upper Midwest.* Minneapolis, MN: University of Minnesota. Upper Midwest Economic Study.

Bourne, Larry. 1980. "Alternative Perspectives on Urban Decline and Population Deconcentration." *Urban Geography* 1: 39-52.

Britnell, G.E. 1939. *The Wheat Economy.* Toronto: University of Toronto Press.

Bruner, E.D. 1936. "Do Villages Grow?" *Rural Sociology* 1: 506-9.

Census of Canada. Census data for 1961, 1971, 1976, 1981, 1986. Ottawa, Ontario: Queen's Printer, various years.

Dacey, Michael F. 1979. "A Growth Process for Zipf's and Yule's City-Size Laws." *Environment and Planning A* 1: 361-72.

Dun and Bradstreet. *Reference Book*. Toronto, Ontario: Dun and Bradstreet, quarterly.

Dunn, Edgar S., Jr. 1980. *The Development of the U.S. Urban System*, two volumes. Baltimore, MD: Johns Hopkins University Press for Resources for the Future.

Fischer, Manfred M. and Peter Nijkamp. 1988. "The Role of Small Firms for Regional Revitalization." *Annals of Regional Science* 12: 28-42.

Fowke, V.C. 1957. *The National Policy and the Wheat Economy*. Toronto: University of Toronto Press.

Fugitt, Glen. 1971. "The Places Left Behind: Population Trends and a Policy for Rural Areas." *Rural Sociology* 36: 449-70.

Furtan, W.H. and G.E. Lee. 1977. "Economic Development of the Saskatchewan Wheat Economy." *Canadian Journal of Agricultural Economics* 25: 15-28.

Hansen, Niles. 1989. "Endogenous Growth Centres: Small Towns and Flexible Production Systems in Rural Denmark." Paper presented at the Symposium on Economic Development and Diversification in Rural Saskatchewan, Saskatoon, 29 November-1 December 1989.

Hart, John F., Neil E. Salisbury, and Everett G. Smith, Jr. 1968. "The Dying Village and Some Notions of Urban Growth." *Economic Geography* 44: 343-49.

Hodge, Gerald. 1965. "The Prediction of Trade Center Viability in the Great Plains." *Papers, Regional Science Association* 15: 87-115.

———. 1968. "Urban Structure and Regional Development." *Papers, Regional Science Association* 21: 101-23.

Lively, C.E. 1932. Growth and Decline of Farm Trade Centres in Minnesota, 1905-1930. Minnesota AES Bulletin 287. St. Paul.

Mackintosh, W.A. 1934. *Prairie Settlement*. Toronto: Macmillan.

Malecki, Edward J. 1988. "New Firm Start-Ups: Key to Rural Growth." *Rural Development Perspectives* 4(2): 18-23.

Martin, Chester and Arthur S. Morton. 1938. *History of Prairie Settlement and 'Dominion Lands' Policy*. Toronto: Macmillan.

Mitchell, J., H.C. Moss and J.S. Clayton. 1944. *Soil Survey of Southern Saskatchewan*. Saskatoon, Saskatchewan: University of Saskatchewan, College of Agriculture, 1944. Soil Survey Report No. 12.

Mulligan, Gordon F. 1981. "The Urbanization Ratio and the Rank-Size Distribution: A Comment." *Journal of Regional Science* 3(21): 283-85.

———. 1984. "Agglomeration and Central Place Theory: A Review of the Literature." *International Regional Science Review* 9: 1-42.

Orloci, L. 1967. "An Agglomerative Method for Classification of Plant Communities." *Journal of Ecology* 55: 193-206.

Parr, John B. 1969. "City Hierarchies and the Distribution of City Size: A Reconsideration of Beckmann's Contribution." *Journal of Regional Science* 9: 239-53.

———. 1970. "Models of City Size in an Urban System." *Papers, Regional Science Association* 25: 221-53.

———. 1978. "Models of the Central Place System: A More General Approach." *Urban Studies* 15: 35-49.

———. 1979. "Regional Economic Change and Regional Spatial Structure: Some Interrelationships." *Environment and Planning A* 11: 825-37.

———. 1980. "Frequency Distributions of Central Places in Southern Germany: A Further Analysis." *Economic Geography* 56: 141-54.

Parr, John B. and K. Suzuki. 1972. "Settlement Populations and the Lognormal Distribution." *Urban Studies* 10: 335-52.

Phillips, W.G. 1956. *The Agricultural Implement Industry in Canada.* Toronto: University of Toronto Press.

Saskatchewan. 1957. Royal Commission on Agriculture and Rural Life. *Service Centres.* Regina, Saskatchewan: Queen's Printer, 1957.

Scott, A.J. 1986. "Industrial Organization and Location: Division of Labor, the Firm, and Spatial Process." *Economic Geography* 62(3): 214-31.

Simon, Herbert A. 1955. "On a Class of Skew Distribution Functions." *Biometrika* 42: 425-40.

SPSS Inc. 1983. *User's Guide.* Chicago: SPSS Inc.

Stabler, Jack C. 1987. "Trade Center Evolution in the Great Plains." *Journal of Regional Science* 27: 225-44.

Stabler, Jack C. and Peter R. Williams. 1973. *The Dynamics of a System of Central Places.* Reading, U.K.: University of Reading. Geographical Papers No. 22.

Statistics Canada. 1991a. *Census of Agriculture, and Ag-Pop. Linked Data Base, 1981 and 1986.* Special tabulations.

———. 1991b. *Census of Population, 1981.* Special tabulations.

White, Roger W. 1974. "Sketches of a Dynamic Central Place Theory." *Economic Geography* 50: 219-27.

———. 1977. "Dynamic Central Place Theory: Results of a Simulation Approach." *Geographic Analysis* 9: 226-43.

———. 1978. "The Simulation of Central Place Dynamics: Two Sector Systems and the Rank-Size Distribution." *Geographical Analysis* 10: 201-8.

Wishart, D. 1987. *Clustan User Manual,* 4th Edition. Edinburgh, U.K.: Edinburgh University.

———. 1982. "Temporal Change in a Central Place System." *Environment and Planning A* 13: 97-118.